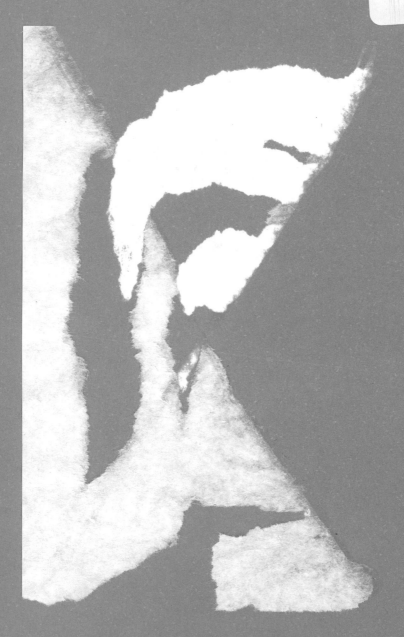

# little hands
# WATER

## Rachel Matthews

Chrysalis Children's Books

We use water for washing, heating, cooking and keeping clean.

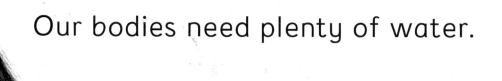

Our bodies need plenty of water.

What does water look like?

What does it taste like?

3

The world's water comes in many forms.
Clouds, rain and snow are made of water.

Water forms streams, lakes, rivers and oceans.

Scoop up a handful of water and try holding it.

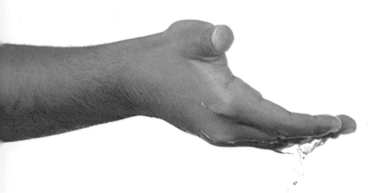

What happens?

What sounds
can you make
with water?

Collect some empty containers.
How many cupfuls of water does it take
to fill each one?

Pour water into
an empty bucket.

Try lifting
the bucket.
How does
it feel?

Wash your hands.
What happens to the water on your skin?

Try pouring
some water
onto different
materials.

What do
you notice?

11

Drop objects like these into some water.

Which of them float and which sink?

Have you ever sat in a boat floating on water?

Sometimes we mix things with water.

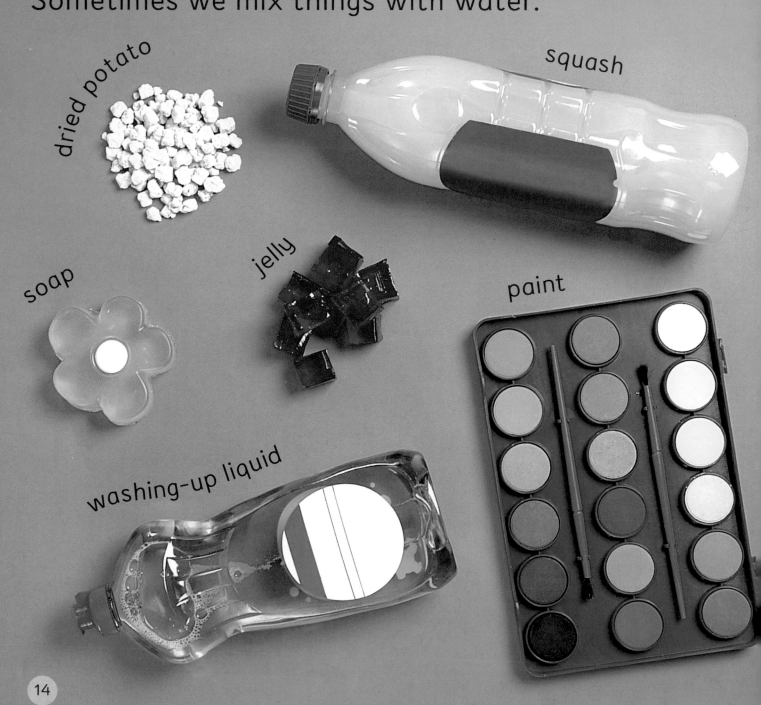

dried potato

squash

soap

jelly

paint

washing-up liquid

Some things don't mix
with water.

Try mixing oil and water.
What do you notice?

When water gets hot enough, it turns to steam.

Make some steam. Ask an adult to boil some water. Stand well back! Watch what happens.

When water gets cold enough, it turns to ice.

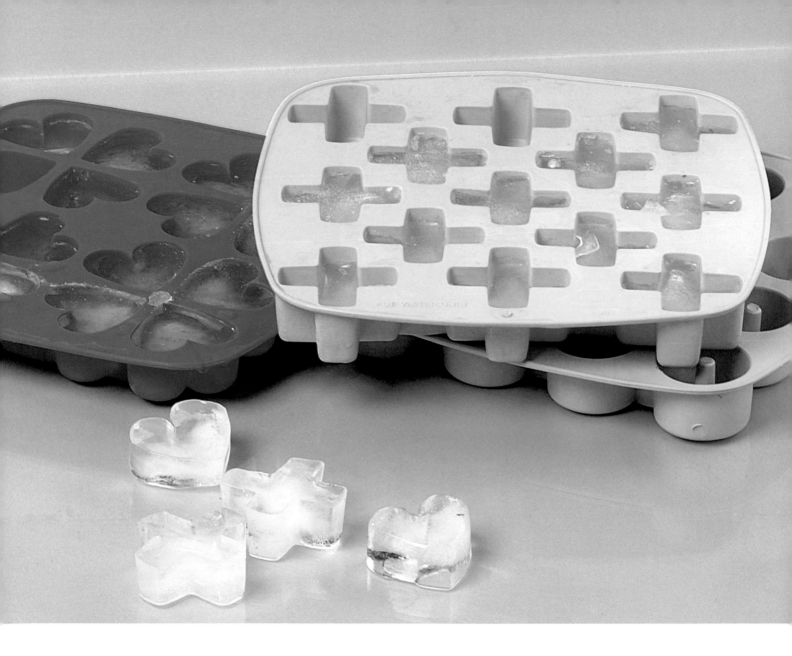

Make some ice. Pour water into some
containers and freeze them.

All living things need water to survive.

We use water in many different ways.
Water is an important part of our lives.

Make a picture all
about water.

# Notes for teachers and parents

## Pages 2–3

**Activity:** Compile a list of the ways in which children come into contact with water every day, including the machines around them that use water (eg. washing machines and steam irons).
**Discussion:** Encourage the children to develop good hygiene practices, such as flushing the loo then washing their hands.

## Pages 4–5

Talking about the children's experience of water in its various forms can foster a sense of wonder about its amazing properties. The children may have been caught in a torrential downpour, be learning to swim or have watched snow blanket the ground.
**Activity:** Through different media, find ways to illustrate the power of moving water, such as in a tidal wave, a waterfall or a tropical storm. On a globe, point out the oceans to show how much of the Earth's surface is covered in water.

## Pages 6–7

When setting up equipment for water play, position the trays at different heights to suit the range of children.
**Discussion:** Discuss the rules for water play, eg. wearing aprons, taking turns or not splashing people. Talk about why each rule is important, making links with the properties of water.
**Activity:** Experiment with ways to make different sounds with water. You could compose a class poem associated with those sounds, eg. drip, splash, whoosh, roar.
**Activity:** Introduce the term 'liquid' and encourage the children to notice how water behaves when they scoop it up in their cupped hands, running downwards through their fingers.

## Pages 8–9

With a variety of transparent containers children can see how water behaves (you could colour the water with a vegetable dye for extra clarity).
**Activity:** Water play is an ideal way to introduce the concept of capacity. The children could count how many cups or spoonfuls of water it takes to fill up a given container, then compare results. Items with hollow handles are useful to illustrate how water will fill any space into which it is poured.

**Activity:** Demonstrate that water is heavy by comparing the weight of an empty bucket and the same bucket full of water.

## Pages 10-11

**Activity:** Experiment with absorbency – compare absorbent materials with waterproof ones.

## Pages 12-13

**Activity:** Illustrate the importance of an object's shape to whether or not it will float by dropping a ball of plasticine into a tank of water, then moulding the same piece into a boat shape and testing whether it will float. What makes it sink?

## Pages 14-15

**Activity:** Introduce the idea that certain substances such as sugar will dissolve in water. The children could experiment with adding differing amounts of water to powder paint and trying out on paper the effects they can achieve with the resulting mixtures.

## Pages 16-17

**Activity:** Illustrate the process of evaporation, by putting damp clothes (eg. wet gloves) on a radiator and seeing how long they take to dry. Explain that the liquid water heats up and changes into a gas called water vapour.

## Pages 18-19

**Activity:** Make ice lollies by pouring diluted fruit squash into moulds and freezing them. Leaving one to melt in a warm place will illustrate a reversible change from solid to liquid water.

## Pages 20-21

Tell the children that water makes up more than half (65%) of our bodies. It's an amazing substance that has no colour, taste or smell and without it no living thing can survive.
**Activity:** To illustrate this you could provide two potted plants and show the children what happens when one is watered regularly and the soil in the other pot is left to dry out.
**Activity:** Provide pictures cut from magazines showing how different people around the world use water from which the children can make a collage.

# Index

First published in the UK in 2005 by
Chrysalis Children's Books
An imprint of Chrysalis Books Group Plc
The Chrysalis Building, Bramley Road
London W10 6SP

Copyright © Chrysalis Books Group Plc 2005

All rights reserved.

ISBN 1 84458 174 8

British Library Cataloguing in Publication Data for this book is available from the British Library.

Associate publisher  Joyce Bentley
Project manager and editor  Penny Worm
Art director  Sarah Goodwin
Designer  Patricia Hopkins
Picture researchers  Veneta Bullen, Miguel Lamas
Photographer  Ray Moller
The author and publishers would like to thank the following people for their contributions to this book: Ruth Thomson, Nikhita Chadda and Mollie Worms.

Printed in China

10 9 8 7 6 5 4 3 2 1

Typography  Natascha Frensch
Read Regular, READ SMALLCAPS and Read Space; European Community
Design Registration 2003 and Copyright © Natascha Frensch 2001-2004
Read Medium, **Read Black** and *Read Slanted* Copyright © Natascha Frensch 2003-2004

READ™ is a revolutionary new typeface that will enhance children's understanding through clear, easily recognisable character shapes. With its evenly spaced and carefully designed characters, READ™ will help children at all stages to improve their literacy skills, and is ideal for young readers, reluctant readers and especially children with dyslexia.

## Picture acknowledgements
All reasonable efforts have been made to ensure the reproduction of content has been done with the consent of copyright owners. If you are aware of any unintentional omissions please contact the publishers directly so that any necessary corrections may be made for future editions.
Corbis: Michael DeYoung 13, Greg Probst 16, Dean Coger 18; Getty Images: Wayne Levin 3; Papilio: Jaime Harron FC (TL), 4, Robert Gill 21.